Changing of Seasons
Four Reflections on Life's Seasons
Charles E. Cravey

In His Steps Publishing Company

ISBN: 978-1-58535-116-9

ISBN: 978-1-58535-117-6

LIBRARY OF CONGRESS CATALOG NUMBER: 2025917150

Cover by Charles E. Cravey and Book Brush.

Printed in the United States of America.

Published by In His Steps Publishing, Statesboro, Georgia.

Contents

Preface

There is a rhythm to life that echoes the turning of the seasons—each one a chapter in the soul's unfolding story. Spring brings renewal. Summer radiates joy. Autumn whispers wisdom, and Winter invites reflection. In these pages, I've sought to capture the spiritual cadence of these seasons, not merely as weathered changes, but as metaphors for the human journey.

The inspiration for this book came one quiet morning at **First United Methodist Church in Statesboro, Georgia**, during a sermon by **Reverend Mark Burgess** entitled *"Take Me with You."* His message, drawn from **Psalm 119:9–16, 105**, stirred something deep within me—a longing to walk more intentionally with God through every season of life. The psalmist's words, "Your word is a lamp to my feet and a light to my path," became a guiding light for this work.

Changing of Seasons is a devotional companion for those navigating transitions—whether blooming, burning bright, letting go, or waiting in stillness. Through Scripture, story, and reflection, I hope to offer readers a sense of belonging in every season and a reminder that God's presence is constant, even as the scenery shifts.

This book is not a roadmap but a fireside invitation. Come sit with me awhile. Let's trace the fingerprints of grace across the calendar of our lives.

With gratitude and hope,
Charles Edward Cravey
August 2025

Chapter 1

The Metaphor of Seasons

The metaphor of seasons serves as a powerful framework for exploring life experiences, growth, and spiritual journeys. Each season represents distinct phases in our lives, highlighting the cyclical nature of existence and the transformation we undergo over time.

In this metaphorical landscape, we find guidance and wisdom that can help us navigate the ups and downs we inevitably encounter. By aligning ourselves with the seasons, we can better understand the natural ebb and flow of life, accepting that each phase, whether filled with joy or challenge, contributes to our personal evolution.

Spring, for instance, invites us to embrace new beginnings with hope and enthusiasm, encouraging us to plant the seeds of our dreams and nurture them into reality. Summer, with its vibrant energy, allows us to revel in the abundance around us, fostering connections and celebrating the progress we have made. As autumn arrives, we are reminded to reflect on our journey, to let go of what no longer serves us, and to gather wisdom from our past experiences. Finally, winter offers an opportunity for introspection and rest, a time to conserve energy and prepare for the renewal that spring will inevitably bring.

By appreciating the lessons each season imparts, we can cultivate resilience and find meaning in the cycles of change that define our lives. This seasonal metaphor not only enriches our understanding of personal growth but also encourages us to live in harmony with the world around us, acknowledging that every ending is but a prelude to a new beginning.

Spring symbolizes renewal, hope, and new beginnings. It reflects moments in our lives when we experience awak-

ening—whether it's starting a new job, beginning a relationship, or embarking on a personal quest. Just as nature
bursts forth with life in the spring, we, too, can embrace
fresh opportunities, nurture our aspirations, and cultivate
our dreams. This season teaches us the importance of
patience and perseverance as we plant seeds that will
grow into something beautiful.

I remember one spring morning in Georgia, the dew still
clinging to the dogwood petals, when my granddaughter
asked why the trees 'wake up so slowly.' Her question
lingered with me. Isn't that how our own awakenings
unfold—quietly, patiently, until the light finds us?

*"Spring does not shout—it whispers. It coaxes the soul
from slumber with the scent of jasmine and the promise
of possibility."*

Spring encourages us to look forward with optimism, to
trust in the potential of our efforts, and to celebrate the
small victories along the way. It reminds us that growth
takes time and that the journey itself is as important as the
destination. As we embark on this path of renewal, we are
invited to be curious, to explore the world with a sense

of wonder, and to allow our creativity to flourish. By embracing the spirit of spring, we learn to welcome change with open arms, understanding that each new beginning is a chance to transform and redefine ourselves.

Summer represents warmth, vitality, and abundance. It is a time of joy, celebration, and flourishing. In this phase, we often find ourselves fully engaged in our pursuits, enjoying the fruits of our labor and basking in the love of those around us. Summer encourages us to savor these moments of growth and connection, reminding us to appreciate the richness of life while also urging us to share our blessings and contribute to the world around us.

As the sun shines brightest in this season, we are inspired to express our true selves and to take bold steps in the direction of our dreams. The long, sun-drenched days invite us to stretch beyond our comfort zones, to explore new horizons, and to nurture our relationships with those we hold dear. This vibrant period is a celebration of life's abundance, an opportunity to embrace gratitude for all that we have achieved.

One summer, I watched a neighbor's garden bloom with wild tomatoes and sunflowers. He shared his harvest with anyone who passed by. That simple act reminded me that abundance is not measured by what we keep, but by what we give away.

"Summer is the season of legacy in motion—when the seeds we planted in faith begin to feed others."

Summer teaches us the value of community and collaboration, encouraging us to lift each other up and to engage in shared experiences that enrich our lives. It is a reminder that, while personal achievements are significant, the joy of giving and connecting with others can be equally rewarding. The lessons of summer inspire us to cultivate a spirit of generosity, to offer our support and kindness, and to create a ripple effect of positivity.

As we revel in the warmth and vitality of summer, we are also reminded of the transient nature of these moments. By living mindfully and cherishing each day, we learn to balance our pursuit of goals with the simple pleasures of the present. Summer invites us to be present, to savor the sweetness of life, and to find joy in both the extraordinary and the everyday.

In embracing the essence of summer, we are encouraged to reflect on the fullness of our lives and to carry this sense of abundance into the seasons that follow, knowing that each phase holds its own unique beauty and lessons.

Autumn symbolizes change, transition, and reflection. As leaves turn vibrant colors and begin to fall, we are prompted to evaluate our lives and acknowledge the impermanence of our experiences. This season often brings both a sense of letting go and a time of gathering insights from the past. It is an opportunity to celebrate our accomplishments while also preparing for the quieter, introspective times ahead. Autumn teaches us resilience and the importance of releasing what no longer serves us on our journey.

In this reflective season, we are encouraged to pause and take stock of our lives, to assess what we have learned and how we have grown. The crisp air and shorter days invite us to slow down, to appreciate the beauty in change, and to find comfort in the familiar rhythms of life. Autumn is a time for gratitude, for acknowledging the richness of our experiences, and for cherishing the memories we have created.

An old letter was tucked inside a family Bible, written by my mother during a difficult autumn in her life. Her words—full of sorrow and hope—taught me that letting go is not forgetting but honoring what shaped us.

"Autumn is the storyteller's season. Each falling leaf carries a tale of what was, and what might still be."

This season also inspires us to embrace the art of letting go, understanding that holding on too tightly to the past can hinder our progress. By releasing outdated habits and beliefs, we create space for new opportunities and insights to emerge. Autumn encourages us to trust in the natural progression of life, to have faith that each ending paves the way for a new beginning.

As we gather the harvest of our efforts, both literal and metaphorical, we are reminded of the cycles that sustain us and the wisdom that comes from understanding our place within them. Autumn teaches us to balance reflection with action, urging us to prepare for the future while savoring the present. It is a season of transformation, where we can find strength in vulnerability and courage in change.

By embracing autumn's lessons, we learn to navigate the transitions in our lives with grace and poise, acknowledging that every phase holds its own beauty and significance. In doing so, we prepare ourselves for the restorative quietude of winter, knowing that our journey of growth and self-discovery continues with each turn of the seasons.

Winter embodies rest, solitude, and contemplation. Just as nature retreats to conserve energy, we too may face periods of introspection and stillness. Winter reminds us to embrace self-care and reflection, recognizing that growth often occurs beneath the surface during times of dormancy. This season is essential for restoration, allowing us to recharge our spirits and prepare for the next cycle of growth.

In the quietude of winter, we find the space to turn inward, to listen to the whispers of our inner voice, and to reconnect with our core values and desires. It is a time to honor the need for rest, understanding that taking a step back is crucial for our well-being and future endeavors. The serene beauty of a winter landscape, with its blanket of snow and stark branches, serves as a reminder of the simplicity and clarity that can be found in moments of stillness.

During a quiet winter retreat, I sat by a frozen lake and watched the stillness settle over the water. It was then I realized that silence is not empty—it's full of answers waiting to be heard.

"Winter is the sacred hush before the hallelujah. It teaches us that rest is not retreat, but preparation."

Winter encourages us to embrace solitude not as loneliness, but as an opportunity for deeper self-discovery and healing. We are invited to explore our inner landscapes, to reflect on our journey thus far, and to set intentions for the path ahead. This season teaches us the importance of patience, reminding us that even when progress seems halted, valuable transformations are happening within.

As we gather warmth from our inner reserves, winter challenges us to cultivate resilience and to find comfort in our own company. It is a time to nurture our creativity, to indulge in quiet pursuits that bring us joy, and to foster a sense of peace and contentment. By embracing the lessons of winter, we learn to trust in the natural rhythms of life, assured that this period of rest is laying the groundwork for the vibrant renewal that spring will bring.

In celebrating the gifts of winter, we come to appreciate the balance and harmony that each season brings to our lives. Just as nature cycles through its phases, we too are part of a grander tapestry, where each moment of quietude and reflection contributes to our ongoing journey of growth and self-discovery.

The metaphor of seasons serves as a mirror to our souls, illustrating that life is a tapestry woven with various experiences, emotions, and lessons. Each season, with its unique characteristics and challenges, contributes to our overall journey, allowing us to evolve, learn, and grow spiritually. By understanding and embracing this cyclical nature, we can find peace in the changes of life and appreciate our own personal transformations as we navigate our way through life.

By aligning ourselves with these natural rhythms, we gain insight into the delicate balance between holding on and letting go, between action and reflection. This awareness brings resilience and perspective, helping us to approach each phase of life with grace and openness. We are reminded that every moment, whether filled with light or shadow, is integral to our development and understanding.

The seasons teach us that impermanence is an inherent part of existence, encouraging us to seek beauty in the present and to cherish the fleeting moments that color our lives. They invite us to dance with the ebb and flow of life, to celebrate our victories, and to find meaning in our challenges. Through this metaphor, we learn to honor the passage of time and to trust in the journey, knowing that each season offers its own gifts and wisdom.

As we embrace the lessons of the seasons, we are inspired to live authentically and to cultivate a deep connection with ourselves and the world around us. This journey of growth and transformation is a testament to the resilience of the human spirit, a reminder that we are all part of a larger, ever-evolving story. In this way, the metaphor of seasons not only enriches our understanding of life but also empowers us to approach our path with courage, gratitude, and hope.

Scriptural Foundations: Introducing Psalm 119 and Leviticus

The exploration of spiritual and moral growth is a journey deeply rooted in scriptural wisdom. Among the many texts within the Bible, Psalm 119 and the book of Leviticus offer profound insights into how divine principles can guide our lives. These scriptures not only provide a foundation for understanding God's law but also encourage intimacy with His word, fostering development in both character and spirituality.

By delving into these texts, we gain a greater appreciation for the divine blueprint that shapes our moral and spiritual journey. Psalm 119, with its poetic devotion to God's word, serves as a reminder that scripture is not merely a set of rules but a source of light and wisdom that illuminates our path. It calls us to cherish and internalize these teachings, allowing them to transform our hearts and minds.

I first encountered Psalm 119 as a young man, searching for direction. Its verses became a lantern in my hand, guiding me through seasons of doubt and renewal.

Similarly, Leviticus, often viewed through the lens of its detailed laws and rituals, reveals the profound connection between holiness and everyday life. Through its guidance, we learn that spiritual growth involves a commitment to living in alignment with divine values, reflecting God's character in our actions and interactions.

Together, Psalm 119 and Leviticus teach us that the pursuit of holiness is a continual process, one that requires dedication, introspection, and a willingness to be molded by God's word. As we engage with these scriptures, we are challenged to cultivate a life of integrity and compassion, inspired by the timeless truths they impart. This journey, underpinned by faith and obedience, leads us toward a deeper relationship with God and a more profound understanding of our place within His creation.

Psalm 119: The Heart of God's Law

Psalm 119 stands as the longest chapter in the Bible, celebrating the beauty and authority of God's word. This psalm is structured as an acrostic poem, with each section beginning with a successive letter of the Hebrew alphabet, emphasizing the wholeness and completeness of God's commandments.

The central theme of Psalm 119 revolves around the psalmist's profound love for God's law. Phrases like "I have hidden your word in my heart" (Psalm 119:11) and "Your word is a lamp to my feet" (Psalm 119:105) reveal a deep-seated belief that scripture illuminates life's pathways, provides wisdom, and leads to moral integrity. The psalmist expresses that true fulfillment and joy are found in obedience to God's statutes, highlighting how adherence to His word fosters spiritual growth and a deeper relationship with the divine.

The psalmist's devotion to God's law is portrayed through a heartfelt dialogue with the divine, where every verse resonates with sincerity and longing for spiritual enlightenment. Psalm 119 serves as an intimate reflection on the transformative power of scripture, encouraging believers to internalize God's teachings and make them an integral part of their daily lives.

This psalm is not merely an ode to the law but a testament to the personal journey of faith and understanding. It emphasizes that engaging with God's word is a dynamic process, one that shapes our thoughts, actions, and identities. The psalmist's repeated affirmations of love for the law illustrate a deep, abiding commitment to living a life aligned with divine principles.

Moreover, Psalm 119 underscores the importance of perseverance and patience in the pursuit of spiritual wisdom. It acknowledges the challenges and struggles one may face on this path, yet it reassures us that steadfastness in faith yields profound rewards. By meditating on God's word, the psalmist finds strength, comfort, and direction, demonstrating that scripture is a source of enduring hope and guidance.

In essence, Psalm 119 invites readers to embark on their own journey of discovery, encouraging them to seek a closer connection with God through His word. It inspires a life of devotion and integrity, reminding us that the pursuit of holiness is a continual, evolving process. Through this psalm, we are called to cherish the timeless wisdom of scripture, allowing it to illuminate our paths and transform our hearts.

Leviticus: The Call to Holiness

In contrast, the book of Leviticus may seem daunting with its laws and regulations; however, it plays a pivotal role in teaching the ancient Israelites—and readers today—about holiness and community life. Positioned within the Torah, Leviticus outlines the moral, ceremonial, and ethical codes necessary for a people set apart for God.

The call to holiness is arguably the heart of Leviticus, epitomized in verses like Leviticus 19:2: "You shall be holy, for I the Lord your God am holy." This call emphasizes that moral and spiritual growth involves aligning oneself with the character of God. Through various offerings, festivals, and dietary laws, Leviticus illustrates how the Israelites were to reflect God's purity in every aspect of life.

Moreover, the book speaks to the communal aspect of faith, highlighting that individual holiness contributes to the greater moral health of the community. This notion encourages readers to think beyond personal righteousness, considering how their actions affect those around them.Through its meticulous attention to detail, Leviticus underscores the interconnectedness of personal and communal holiness, reminding us that our spiritual journey is not undertaken in isolation. Each law and ritual serves as a tangible expression of faith, demonstrating how everyday actions are infused with spiritual significance.

Leviticus also highlights the importance of justice and compassion in community life. The directives concerning care for the poor, fair treatment of workers, and honesty in business dealings reveal a profound commitment to social ethics. These principles encourage us to build communities grounded in equity and love, reflecting the divine character in our interactions with others.

The book challenges us to consider the broader implications of holiness, extending beyond ritual observance to encompass acts of kindness, integrity, and respect for all of creation. In doing so, Leviticus invites us to embody a holistic vision of faith, where spiritual devotion is seamlessly integrated with ethical living.

By engaging with Leviticus, we are called to examine the ways in which our own lives can mirror the divine attributes of mercy and justice. This call to holiness is an ongoing journey, inviting us to continually refine our character and deepen our commitment to living out God's values in every facet of life.

Leviticus serves as a powerful reminder that the pursuit of holiness is both a personal and collective endeavor. It encourages us to seek a life that honors God through our actions and to contribute to a community that reflects His love and righteousness. As we strive to live according to these principles, we are inspired to create a world that embodies the sacred harmony envisioned in these ancient texts.

Conclusion

Both Psalm 119 and Leviticus remind us that moral and spiritual growth is a dynamic process grounded in the study and application of God's word. Psalm 119 invites us into a loving relationship with scripture, celebrating its transformative power in our lives. Meanwhile, Leviticus challenges us to live in a way that reflects holiness, shaping our communities along the way. Together, these texts guide us to a deeper understanding of what it means to grow spiritually and morally in a world that often challenges those ideals. Through engaging with these scriptures, believers are encouraged to seek God's guidance as they navigate their paths, fostering a life marked by integrity, purpose, and divine connection.

As we embrace the lessons from both Psalm 119 and Leviticus, we are reminded that our spiritual journey is not one of isolation but a shared experience within the broader tapestry of community and faith. Each step, guided by the wisdom of scripture, encourages us to embody the virtues of compassion, justice, and humility, creating ripples of positive change in the world around us.

In this pursuit, we are called to be beacons of light, reflecting the divine love and wisdom that these sacred texts offer. By internalizing their teachings, we cultivate resilience and find the courage to face life's challenges with grace and conviction. Our growth, both moral and spiritual, becomes a testament to the enduring power of faith and the transformative impact of living in harmony with God's principles.

The journey through Psalm 119 and Leviticus is an invitation to live authentically, to engage deeply with our beliefs, and to commit to a life that honors the sacred trust bestowed upon us. As we continue to explore these profound texts, may we be inspired to nurture our spiritual growth, enrich our communities, and contribute to a world that reflects the beauty and harmony envisioned in God's word.

Chapter 2

The Season of Spring

New Beginnings

As the world awakens from its wintry slumber, spring emerges as a vibrant metaphor for birth, renewal, and hope. The delicate buds of flowers brave their way through previously frozen earth, exhibiting the resilience inherent in nature—a testament to the beauty of new beginnings. Just as the days grow longer and warmer, our lives also invite the potential for transformation and rejuvenation.

The air is filled with a gentle hum of anticipation, as if the universe itself is holding its breath in eager expectation of the wonders to come. Each morning, the sun rises a little earlier, casting a golden glow over the world and coaxing it back to life. Birds return from their long migrations, filling the air with their melodious symphony, a harbinger of the season's promise. This awakening is not just confined to the natural world; it resonates within us too, stirring a desire to shed the layers of complacency and embrace the fresh start that spring symbolizes.

"One swallow does not make a spring, nor does one fine day." —Aristotle

In this chapter, we will explore how this season of renewal can inspire us to embark on new journeys, whether in personal growth, relationships, or creative endeavors. The gentle unfolding of spring serves as a powerful reminder that change, though sometimes daunting, is an essential part of life's journey. It encourages us to step out of our comfort zones and into the fertile ground of potential, where dreams can take root and aspirations blossom into reality.

As we delve into the stories and lessons that spring offers, let us carry its spirit of optimism and courage with us. Let us be like the flowers that reach toward the sun, unafraid of the challenges that lie ahead, confident in our ability to grow and thrive. In the season of spring, may we find the inspiration to begin anew, with hearts open to the myriad possibilities that await.

I remember one spring afternoon as a boy in Georgia, chasing butterflies through a field of clover. My mother watched me from the porch, humming a hymn. That moment—simple, fleeting—planted in me a lifelong reverence for beauty, for grace in motion.

The Metaphor of Spring

Spring embodies more than just a change in the weather; it symbolizes a profound rebirth. This season teaches us that endings are often disguised as beginnings. The barren branches of winter give way to lush greenery, reminding us that we can shed our past self to embrace new opportunities. In our lives, each day can usher in the chance to start again—be it through career shifts, new relationships, or spiritual awakening.

Take, for instance, the journey of starting a new career. It often begins with uncertainty and fear—the chilling remnants of winter's desolation. Yet, as one ventures into unfamiliar territory, the excitement of possibility blooms like wildflowers in a meadow. Every new journey is akin to planting a seed, and with patience and care, we nurture it until it grows into something beautiful and fruitful.

"Men swarmed about the body, as flies that buzz round the full milk-pails in the season of spring."
—*Homer (Iliad)*

One may also encounter the exhilarating yet daunting experience of forming new relationships. The hesitance to open oneself up can feel like the last frost of the season, but the warmth of connection can transform that fear into vulnerability. These bonds, when nurtured, flourish and enhance our lives, just as the spring sun coaxes blossoms from their buds.

It was during a spring retreat that a mentor once told me, "Charles, the soil of your soul is ready. Plant what matters." His words stayed with me, especially when I began mentoring others. Spring reminds us that encouragement is a form of sowing.

The metaphor of spring extends into the realm of personal growth, where spiritual awakenings mirror nature's revival. As we let go of the cold grip of doubt and embrace warmth and optimism, our spirits are renewed. This renewal is not merely an external transformation but an internal one, offering a deeper understanding of ourselves and our place in the world.

Moreover, spring's lessons can be found in the pursuit of creative endeavors. Just as a garden requires tending, so too does our creativity. The initial stages of a creative project can be fraught with uncertainty, much like the unpredictable weather that marks the transition from winter to spring. Yet, with perseverance and nurturing, our ideas can blossom into masterpieces.

Spring teaches us the beauty of renewal and the courage to embrace change. It reminds us to be patient with ourselves and to trust in the process of growth. Whether we are cultivating our careers, nurturing relationships, or exploring our spirituality, spring encourages us to lean into the unfolding potential of our lives with hope and determination. As we journey through this season, may we carry its lessons with us, allowing them to inspire and guide us through every chapter of our lives.

Life Experiences: New Beginnings

Reflecting on my own experiences, I recall the spring I decided to embark on a completely foreign path: pursuing my passion for writing. The notion of pouring my heart onto the page both thrilled and terrified me. As I stood on the precipice of this new venture, I felt the exhilaration of possibility dancing in my chest—each word I penned became a step into the vibrant world of creativity. It was my spring—a time of shedding old doubts and embracing a renewed sense of purpose.

"The art of living well and the art of dying well are one."
—Epicurus

Broader themes resonate too: people often share stories of spiritual rebirth in spring. Many experience a rekindling of faith or a newfound connection with spirituality, paralleling nature's revival. This cyclical return not only offers a fresh outlook but also a deeper understanding of self, as personal growth mirrors the unfolding petals of blooming flowers.

The path was not always easy; like any garden, it required patience and nurturing. There were moments of doubt, akin to the chilly spring mornings that remind us of winter's lingering grasp, yet with each sentence crafted, a sense of fulfillment emerged, warming my soul like the sun that steadily climbs higher in the sky. This journey of writing became not just an exploration of language, but a profound journey of self-discovery, revealing layers of creativity I never knew existed.

In conversations with friends and family, I discovered that my experience was not unique. Many shared similar tales of spring-inspired transformations, whether it was starting a new career, embarking on a personal project, or even reaching out to mend fractured relationships. The essence of spring infused these narratives, offering a shared sense of renewal and hope.

"Wait for the wisest of all counselors." —Pericles

Spring, with its promise of new beginnings, acts as a gentle catalyst, encouraging us to take risks and embrace the unfamiliar. It teaches us that while the path may be fraught with challenges, the rewards of perseverance and courage are immense. As I continue my writing journey, I am reminded that each spring offers a chance to reaffirm my commitment to this passion, to nurture my craft, and to allow my creativity to flourish.

My wife and I once planted a garden together, each row a prayer for our children's future. Watching those seeds sprout became a sacred rhythm—an echo of God's quiet work in our lives.

Psalm 1:3—"He is like a tree planted by streams of water, which yields its fruit in season."

In this season of renewal, may we all find the courage to pursue our dreams with vigor and determination. Let us welcome the changes that spring brings, knowing that with every fresh start comes the opportunity for growth and transformation. As we step into the vibrant tapestry of possibilities, may we be inspired by the beauty of spring to write our own stories, filled with hope, resilience, and endless potential.

Isaiah 43:19—"See, I am doing a new thing! Now it springs up; do you not perceive it?"

Scripture Reference: Longing for Guidance

In times of seeking clarity and direction, the Scriptures offer profound wisdom, particularly Psalm 119. Verses within this Psalm reflect a deep longing for guidance—echoing the sentiments often felt in spring when the world feels ripe with possibilities. The verses implore us to seek understanding and illumination through God's word.

Consider verse 105: "Your word is a lamp for my feet, a light on my path." This imagery captures the essence of spring: light piercing through the darkness, guiding us through our newfound paths. Just as the sun's rays melt away the frost, seeking guidance in our moments of longing directs us toward the clarity we crave.

In this season of rejuvenation, we are called to embrace the potential of new beginnings, bolstering our journeys with faith and courage. As we reflect on our pasts and step into the future, let us carry the spirit of spring within us—the hope that with each new dawn, there exists the possibility of growth and renewal. Whether in career, relationship, or spirituality, may we remember that spring is not merely a season, but a state of being, forever inviting us to begin anew.

"Of all possessions, a friend is the most precious."
—Herodotus

When we find ourselves at crossroads, the wisdom of the Scriptures can serve as a compass, gently directing us towards the path that aligns with our true purpose. This pursuit of guidance is akin to the transformative power of spring—both guiding us through transitions and encouraging us to embrace the journey with an open heart.

Song of Solomon 2:11-12—"See! The winter is past; the rains are over and gone. Flowers appear on the earth..."

As we navigate these personal seasons of change, let us draw strength from the enduring lessons of spring and Scripture alike. They remind us that even in moments of uncertainty, there is a guiding light ready to illuminate our way. This harmonious blend of faith and renewal calls us to trust in the process, to nurture our dreams, and to step confidently into the realms of possibility that await.

"A society grows great when old men plant trees whose shade they know they shall never sit in." —Greek Proverb

May we all find solace and inspiration in the gentle whisper of spring's promise, allowing it to awaken within us a deep-seated courage to pursue our dreams and aspirations. As we embark on these journeys, let us be mindful of the wisdom that guides us, ever ready to embrace the new beginnings that each day brings.

What seeds are you planting this spring—in your heart, your home, your creative life?

Blessing:

May this season awaken in you the courage to begin again, the grace to grow slowly, and the faith to believe that what you plant in love will bloom in time.

Sonnet for the Season of Spring

Charles E. Cravey

When winter's hush begins to fade away,

And morning light adorns the waking land,

The buds arise in gentle, green ballet,

As grace and growth extend their quiet hand.

The robin sings a hymn of hope anew,

Its melody a balm for weary hearts.

Each petal dares to drink the sky's soft hue,

As heaven's brush revives what cold departs.

So too the soul, once cloaked in doubt and fear,

Now stirs beneath the warmth of sacred flame.

The Word—a lamp—makes every pathway clear,

And whispers, "Child, begin. You're not the same."

Let spring within you rise, unbound, unashamed—

A garden sown in faith, by love reclaimed.

Chapter 3

The Season of Summer

Growth and Abundance

As we step into the warmth of summer, we find ourselves enveloped in a season that symbolizes vibrancy, growth, and flourishing. Just as the earth bursts forth with life, so too do our spirits awaken to the possibilities of abundance that this time brings. Summer is not merely a season marked by the sun's brilliance; it is a metaphor for the periods in our lives when success and joy flourish, and we experience the richness of our endeavors.

"Let us not grow weary in doing good." —Galatians 6:9

The beauty of summer lies in its potential for growth. This season invites us to reflect on our own life experiences, particularly those moments when we have felt a surge of success and unbounded joy. Remember the times when you accomplished a long-standing goal, when laughter filled the air, and friendships blossomed like flowers in full bloom? Such memories are the fruits of summer, reminders that we possess the capability to thrive in our endeavors, to cultivate our talents, and to blossom into who we are meant to be.

To navigate these seasons of abundance, it is essential to embrace a mindset that is open to growth. Just as the farmer labors in the fields, nurturing plants with care and attention, we too must nurture our dreams with intention. Small, consistent efforts can yield remarkable results. This summer, let us prioritize our passions and engage with our communities, drawing strength and inspiration from one another's growth.

In times of flourishing, it is also vital to remember the beauty of connection. The Levitical laws provide a rich tapestry of how community thrives in celebration. Leviticus 25 introduces the Year of Jubilee—a profound reminder of joy, provision, and communal prosperity. Every fifty years, this year was set aside to restore lands to their original owners and free those who were enslaved. It encouraged the community to come together, celebrating with feasting and thanksgiving as God's blessings overflowed.

"Those who sow in tears shall reap with shouts of joy."
—Psalm 126:5

It had rained hard that morning, the kind of Southern summer storm that leaves the air thick and the ground slick. My grandson, barefoot and bold, darted down the dirt road beside our house with the kind of abandon only children possess. The red Georgia clay had turned to pudding, and before I could call out, he slipped—arms flailing, laughter erupting mid-fall. He landed with a glorious splat, covered head to toe in mud.

I rushed over, half-concerned, half-amused. But before I could speak, he looked up at me with a grin so wide it could've split the sky. "I'm a mud monster!" he declared, arms raised in triumph.

In that moment, I saw the sacredness of surrender. The joy of letting go. The freedom to fall and laugh and be fully present in the mess. It reminded me of Ellie the elephant—clumsy, dreaming, tumbling through life's puddles. And it reminded me of myself, too. That sometimes, the richest growth comes not from staying clean, but from embracing the muddy, messy, grace-filled tumble of life.

As we embrace the spirit of summer in our lives, we can practice the same principles of joy and generosity. The spirit of the Jubilee calls us to revitalize our connections with others, to share our successes, and to support those around us in their journeys. When we come together in a spirit of abundance, we create a ripple effect, where everyone's flourishing contributes to the strength of the whole.

"A gift consists not in what is done or given, but in the intention of the giver." —Seneca

Let this summer be a season of not just personal growth, but also of communal flourishing. As the sun nourishes the earth, let your actions nurture those around you. Celebrate the victories—big and small—of your friends and family. Extend your hand to those in need and share the harvest of your efforts. In this season of growth, may we collectively enter the fullness of joy that comes from understanding that abundance is not just for ourselves, but for everyone within our reach.

"The happiness of your life depends upon the quality of your thoughts." —Marcus Aurelius

In summary, the season of summer invites us into a vibrant tapestry of growth and community. As we reflect on our past successes and prepare for the bountiful moments ahead, let us embody the principles found in the heart of scripture—embracing joy, promoting unity, and celebrating abundance together. In doing so, we can create a life that truly flourishes.

This chapter on summer serves as a beautiful reminder that our lives, much like the seasons, are cyclical. Each phase offers unique opportunities for learning, growth, and renewal. As we bask in the warmth and energy of summer, let us remember to carry its lessons forward into the cooler, quieter seasons that follow. By doing so, we ensure that the vibrancy of summer lives on within us,

fueling our dreams and aspirations no matter the external climate.

May we take this time to sow seeds of kindness and
compassion, knowing that what we plant today will
blossom into tomorrow's blessings. And as the days
grow long and the nights warm, let us revel in the
abundant joys that summer brings, cherishing the connections we foster with those around us. Here's to a
season of growth, gratitude, and the shared journey
towards a future bright with possibility.

May the vibrant spirit of summer inspire us to embrace
each day with open hearts and a sense of wonder. As
we journey through this season, let us take the time
to appreciate the simple pleasures—a leisurely walk in
the park, the laughter shared with friends, or the quiet
moments of reflection under a starlit sky. These experiences are the threads that weave the rich tapestry of
our lives.

Let us also remember that the essence of summer lies not
just in personal achievement, but in the connections we
nurture and the joy we share with others. By supporting
one another and celebrating each other's successes, we
create a community where everyone thrives. This inter-

connectedness is the true gift of summer—a reminder
that we are all part of something greater than ourselves.

"Don't you know yet? It is your light that lights the world."
—Rumi

As we enjoy the golden days of this season, let's commit to
carrying its warmth and generosity into every interaction.
Whether through acts of kindness or words of encouragement, our contributions can light up the world around us.
Here's to embracing the season's bounty, fostering meaningful relationships, and embarking on new adventures
with a spirit of optimism and hope. Let the summer be
a time of joyful abundance for all, guiding us towards a
future filled with endless possibilities.

Blessing:

May you walk boldly into the warmth of summer,

Feet bare, heart open, spirit free.

*May the rains soften your path, and the sun kiss your
shoulders.*

May you find joy in the tumble, grace in the mess,

And laughter that rises like a hymn from the clay.

Go forth, beloved, into the season of abundance—

Mud-splattered, heart-glad, and embraced.

Sonnet of Golden Days

Charles E. Cravey

In summer's glow, the earth brings forth its yield,
With golden days and laughter's gentle cheer.
To tend the seeds of dreams in heart's wide field,
And nurture them with care from year to year.

Rejoicing in the bounty that we share,
A time to give, to bless, to understand.
Of Jubilee, let love beyond compare
In generous spirit, touch both heart and hand.

Let not these moments slip like grains of sand,
For in our light is the world's brightness cast.
Together, harvesting blessings that expand,
And sowing seeds of goodness ever lasts.

As sunlight spills o'er meadows green and bright,
Abundant life unfolds in summer's light.

Chapter 4

The Season of Autumn

Transition and Reflection

Autumn, with its vibrant tapestry of reds, oranges, and yellows, serves as a powerful metaphor for the inevitable changes we face in life. Just as the leaves turn and fall from their branches, we too must embrace the transitions that come our way.

This season beautifully illustrates the necessity of letting go—of relationships, habits, and even dreams that no longer serve us. As we watch the world around us shift, we are called to reflect on our own personal growth.

"To everything there is a season, and a time to every purpose under the heaven." —Ecclesiastes 3:1

In this time of transformation, the gentle rustle of leaves becomes a symphony of change, urging us to listen closely to the whispers of our hearts. Each leaf that drifts to the ground is a poignant reminder that endings pave the way for new beginnings. It is in the quiet moments of autumn that we find the space to breathe deeply, to pause, and to consider the paths we have walked.

This season invites us to reconnect with our inner selves, to evaluate the journey thus far, and to set intentions for the future. It is a time to honor the lessons we have learned, both from our triumphs and our trials. As we walk through the crisp, cool air, we are encouraged to let go of any burdens that weigh us down, making room for the fresh opportunities and experiences that await us.

"Let yourself be silently drawn by the strange pull of what you really love. It will not lead you astray." — Rumi

The beauty of autumn lies not just in its colors but in its gentle reminder of the cyclical nature of life. Just as nature prepares for the quiet dormancy of winter, we too must prepare for the next phases of our lives with grace and courage. In embracing the season of autumn, we find the strength to release what no longer serves us, welcoming the potential for growth and renewal that each new day brings.

The Metaphor of Autumn

In the crisp, cool air of autumn, we find a moment of introspection. The trees, stripped bare, remind us that there is beauty in vulnerability and strength in surrender. Just as the leaves fall to the ground, making way for new growth in the spring, we must release the parts of our lives that hold us back. This act of letting go can often be painful, yet it is essential for progress. Each fallen leaf whispers a reminder that change is necessary for renewal.

"It is only with the heart that one can see rightly; what is essential is invisible to the eye." —Antoine de Saint-Exupery, The Little Prince

Transition, much like the seasonal shifts, forces us to pause and reflect. It offers us the opportunity to assess where we've been and where we are headed. We can analyze our life experiences, understanding that every challenge faced, and every victory achieved, serves as a steppingstone on our journey. In times of transition, it's crucial to cultivate gratitude for the lessons learned—both the enlightening moments and the struggles that shaped us.

By embracing these transitions, we learn to appreciate the impermanence of life and the beauty that comes with each new phase. Autumn, with its vivid colors and gentle reminders of life's cyclical nature, teaches us the art of adaptation. As we witness the natural world preparing for winter, we are inspired to prepare ourselves for whatever lies ahead, armed with the wisdom gained from past experiences.

This season is not just about endings but also about acknowledging the potential that lies within every new beginning. The shedding of leaves becomes a metaphor for shedding our fears, doubts, and hesitations, allowing us to step into the future with renewed hope and determination. Autumn encourages us to embrace our authentic selves, to stand tall and unafraid, much like the trees that remain steadfast despite the starkness of their branches.

As we journey through this season, let us take time to listen to the whispers of the wind and the crunch of leaves underfoot. Let us find joy in the simple pleasures—warm cups of tea, the scent of cinnamon and cloves, and the golden light of late afternoon. These moments remind us to slow down and savor the present, to reflect on how far we've come, and to dream about where we are going.

In this time of reflection, may we find clarity and purpose. Let us open our hearts to the possibility of growth and transformation, trusting that just as autumn leads to winter, it also heralds the promise of spring. With each passing day, we are given the chance to start anew, to write the next chapter of our lives with intention and love.

Life Experiences: Navigating Change

In my own life, I've encountered several seasons of transition. There were moments when I held tightly to familiar routines and relationships, fearing the unknown. However, as I learned to embrace change, I discovered new passions and opportunities. For instance, a career shift that initially felt daunting led me to discover strengths I never knew I had. Each experience served as a reminder that while I may not have control over external circumstances, I do have the power to shape my response.

The importance of reflection during these transitions cannot be overstated. It encourages us to recognize patterns in our life, understand what works, and let go of what does not. I recall a time when I took a long walk in the autumn air, pondering my past decisions. It was during this reflective journey that I found clarity and perspective, leading me to cultivate gratitude for both my triumphs and hardships.

Reflection, much like the vibrant hues of autumn, brings a sense of richness and depth to our lives. It provides us with the opportunity to pause and appreciate the journey thus far, acknowledging both the achievements and the lessons learned along the way. In these moments of introspection, we can identify the areas where we've grown and the paths that have yet to be explored.

Moreover, embracing change with an open heart allows us to tap into our resilience and adaptability. As I ventured into new territories, I realized that each challenge was a steppingstone to personal growth. With every unexpected twist, I gained a deeper understanding of my own capabilities and the strength to face future transitions with confidence.

The beauty of navigating change lies in the discovery of our authentic selves. Much like the trees that shed their leaves, we too must shed the layers that no longer serve us, revealing our true essence. This process, while sometimes uncomfortable, is necessary for us to evolve and flourish.

As I continue to journey through life's seasons, I remind myself to find joy in the present moment. Whether it's the simple pleasure of a warm embrace or the laughter shared with loved ones, these moments of connection ground me and remind me of the beauty that exists in the here and now.

In embracing change and reflection, life is not just about reaching a destination but about savoring each step along the way. I am grateful for the experiences that have shaped me and look forward to the endless possibilities that lie ahead, ever eager to learn, grow, and embrace the new beginnings that each day brings.

Scripture Reference: Learning and Wisdom

The wisdom found in Psalm 119 aligns beautifully with the themes of autumn, offering profound insights into the learning process and growth through challenges. Verses such as Psalm 119:71, "It was good for me to be afflicted so that I might learn your decrees," remind us that even the most challenging times can lead to a deeper understanding of ourselves and our faith.

Moreover, Psalm 119:105 states, "Your word is a lamp for my feet, a light on my path." This scripture emphasizes the importance of guidance as we navigate through life's transitions. Reflection paired with gratitude allows us to see the path illuminated by the lessons learned from our experiences. Just as autumn prepares the world for the renewal of spring, our reflections prepare us for the next chapter of our lives.

In closing, as we find ourselves in the season of autumn—both literally and metaphorically—let us embrace change, engage in meaningful reflection, and cultivate a heart of gratitude for our journey. In doing so, we pave the way for growth, wisdom, and an abundant life ahead.

With every whisper of the wind and every fallen leaf, we are reminded that life is a journey of continuous learning and transformation. Just as the trees prepare silently for the coming winter, we too are encouraged to gather wisdom from the seasons of our lives. In this time of reflection, let us find strength in the knowledge that we are never alone on this path; our experiences, our faith, and the love that surrounds us guide us forward.

"Nature does not hurry, yet everything is accomplished."
—Lao Tzu

I remember sitting on the porch one October evening, the kind where the air smells of woodsmoke and the sky blushes early. A single leaf drifted down and landed on the arm of my rocking chair. It was golden, veined, and brittle at the edges—beautiful in its surrender.

I thought of my brother then. He used to rake leaves in long, deliberate rows, never rushing, always humming. After he passed, I found myself raking in the same rhythm, not to tidy the yard, but to feel close to him. That autumn, as I watched the leaf tremble in the breeze, I realized I had been holding on to grief like a tightly clutched rake. I hadn't let myself feel the fullness of the loss, nor the quiet joy of his memory.

That evening, I let the leaf fall. I let the rake rest. And I whispered a thank-you to the wind—for the love, the lessons, and the letting go.

As we walk through the crisp days of autumn, may we carry with us the hope of spring—the promise that every ending is but a prelude to a new beginning. Let us nurture our spirits with kindness, open our hearts to new possibilities, and step bravely into the future, assured that we are equipped with the wisdom and resilience to embrace whatever lies ahead.

"The falling leaf returns to the root." —Rumi

Blessing:

May the rustle of leaves remind you of the beauty in letting go.

May your heart be lightened by reflection, and your spirit steadied by grace.

May you walk through this season with courage,

Knowing that every ending carries the seed of a beginning.

May the wisdom of autumn settle gently upon you—

A golden hush, a sacred pause, a quiet strength.

Go forth, beloved, into the crisp air of change,

Wrapped in gratitude, rooted in hope, and ready for re-newal.

Sonnet on "The Benediction of Leaves"

Charles E. Cravey

The trees stand bare, yet noble in their grace,

Their golden crowns now scattered on the ground.

Each leaf a whisper from the past we face,

A memory in motion, lost then found.

The wind, a gentle preacher, speaks of change,

Of letting go, of finding strength in fall.

It stirs the soul with truths both deep and strange,

That endings are beginnings, after all.

So let the colors fade, the branches bend,

Let silence settle where the song once played.

For in this hush, the heart begins to mend,

And hope takes root where sorrow once had stayed.

O Autumn, teach us how to yield and grow—

To bless the loss and trust the seeds we sow.

Chapter 5

The Season of Winter

Trials and Resilience

As the frost settles over the landscape, winter's grasp reminds us of nature's ability to retreat into a period of dormancy. Just as the trees stand barren and the earth lies under a blanket of snow, we too experience seasons that feel stark and unyielding. In this chapter, we will explore the metaphor of winter, representing our struggles, solitude, and the endurance we cultivate amid life's harshest trials.

"In the depth of winter, I finally learned that within me there lay an invincible summer." —Albert Camus

Through this exploration, we will uncover how these metaphorical winters can become powerful catalysts for personal growth and transformation.

Winter, with its chilling winds and quiet nights, offers us a unique opportunity to pause and reflect. It is a time when the world slows down, and we are given the chance to look inward, examining the foundations of our strength and the depth of our resilience. This season, though daunting, is an invitation to embrace stillness and find beauty in the quiet moments of introspection.

"The snow goose need not bathe to make itself white. Neither need you do anything but be yourself." —Lao Tzu

In the face of adversity, winter teaches us the art of patience and the importance of nurturing hope. Just as the seeds hidden beneath the frosty soil await the warmth of spring, our inner potential lies dormant, ready to awaken with renewed vigor. It is during these challenging times that we learn to appreciate the subtle comforts—a warm cup of tea, the embrace of a loved one, or the gentle flicker of a candle—that bring light to our darkest days.

As we journey through our personal winters, let us remember that each trial is not just an obstacle, but a steppingstone towards a more profound understanding of ourselves and the world around us. By embracing the season of winter, we allow ourselves to grow in resilience and emerge with a greater capacity for compassion, empathy, and strength.

In the pages to come, we will delve deeper into the stories of those who have weathered their own winters, drawing inspiration from their experiences and discovering the universal truths that bind us all in our shared journey through life's seasons.

The Metaphor of Winter

Winter embodies the trials of life—moments when we find ourselves isolated, battling the cold winds of doubt and despair. It is a time when the vibrant colors of our existence seem muted and the warmth of connection feels distant. However, it is within this stark season that we can uncover the seeds of resilience. The barren branches, devoid of leaves, are not a sign of defeat but an invitation to reflect on our growth beneath the surface.

"No winter lasts forever; no spring skips its turn." —Hal Borland

During my own winter seasons, I have faced numerous challenges—both personal and professional. There were days filled with uncertainty when aspirations felt out of reach, and moments when solitude echoed louder than words of encouragement. Yet, within these struggles, I learned invaluable lessons on perseverance. The winter landscape taught me that enduring the cold, allowing my thoughts to crystallize into clarity, often paved the way for a more profound understanding of myself and my purpose.

In embracing the metaphor of winter, we find a profound symbolism that speaks to the heart of human experience. This season, with its stark beauty and quiet introspection, offers us the chance to cultivate inner strength, much like the hardy evergreens that stand resilient amidst the snow.

As we navigate through life's winters, we must remember that these times of trial are not merely obstacles but opportunities for transformation.

The quietude of winter encourages introspection, urging us to slow down and listen to the whispers of our own hearts. It is a time to nurture our inner selves, to tend to the roots of our being, and to lay the groundwork for future growth. Just as the world outside is stripped bare, revealing the intricate skeletons of trees, we too are invited to shed what no longer serves us, making room for new beginnings.

"Adversity introduces a man to himself." —Albert Einstein

Winter teaches us the value of patience, the importance of conserving energy for the days when we will once again bloom. It reminds us that beneath the snow, life is preparing to burst forth with renewed vigor. In our own lives, this season of dormancy is a time to gather strength, to dream of the possibilities that await us when the thaw comes.

As the cold winds blow, let us wrap ourselves in the warmth of hope, knowing that this season, like all others, is part of the cycle of life. We are not alone in our winters;

the stories of those who have walked this path before us offer guidance and inspiration. Let us draw from their wisdom and courage, finding solace in the knowledge that spring will return, bringing with it the promise of renewal and the joy of new beginnings.

"The wound is the place where the Light enters you."
—Rumi

Life Experiences: Hardship and Doubt

In the darkest nights, when doubt loomed large, I found myself drawing strength from experiences that had tested my resolve. One winter, I lost a job that had defined my professional identity, leaving me questioning my capabilities. It was a time void of warmth, where the future felt uncertain and seemingly bleak. Yet, in this solitude, I grasped the essential lesson that hardship is often a precursor to growth. Just as the earth lies still in winter, waiting for spring's nurturing touch, I learned to hold space for my own evolution.

Another winter, I faced personal loss—an event that shattered my understanding of stability. In those moments, the silent weight of grief felt insurmountable. But it was through this profound sorrow that I began to understand the depth of resilience. I discovered that it was okay to lean into the discomfort of my feelings. Just as the world endures harsh winters, my spirit too could withstand the storms, emerging stronger and more compassionate.

In these seasons of hardship, I learned that doubt and uncertainty, though daunting, are not insurmountable. They are the crucibles in which our inner strength is forged. As I navigated these challenging winters, I realized that each trial was an opportunity to redefine my narrative, to reclaim my sense of purpose, and to cultivate a deeper empathy for both myself and others.

During these times, I found solace in the small comforts—the quiet moments of reflection, the gentle support of friends, and the unwavering love of family. These became my guiding lights, illuminating the path forward even when the way seemed obscured by the shadows of doubt.

Moreover, these personal winters taught me the importance of community and connection. Just as the trees stand together, their roots intertwined beneath the snow, I discovered the value of leaning on those around me. The shared stories of struggle and triumph became a tapestry of hope and inspiration, reminding me that we are never truly alone in our journeys.

As I reflect on these experiences, I am reminded that the trials we face are not just challenges to be overcome but are integral parts of our growth. They shape us, molding our character and enriching our understanding of the world. In the end, the winters of our lives, while severe, are also seasons of profound transformation, preparing us for the abundant springs that lie ahead.

Scriptural Reflections: Comfort Amidst Trials

In times of need, I sought solace in scripture, finding hope in the words of Psalm 119. Verses that speak of God's faithfulness became a cornerstone for my resilience. One such passage reminds us, "Your word is a lamp for my feet, a light on my path" (Psalm 119:105). In the moments where darkness threatened to consume me, these verses illuminated my way, guiding me through the coldest nights.

Moreover, the encouragement found in verses such as "It is good for me that I was afflicted, that I might learn your statutes" (Psalm 119:71) resonates deeply. This verse reflects the transformative power of trials; each struggle was a lesson, a stepping stone towards a greater understanding of God's plan for my life.

As we dwell in winter's embrace, it becomes imperative to remember that this season is temporary. The promise of spring looms, reminding us that every trial carries within it the promise of renewal. Just as winter prepares the earth for the burgeoning life of spring, our hardships shape us, fostering resilience and character that will bloom anew when the sun returns.

In the trials we face, we are not alone. Like the wayward branches, we can reach toward the light of hope, finding strength in the knowledge that even in the depths of winter, there is the potential for revival, and every struggle can lead us closer to the warmth of our true selves.

During these times, the scriptures have been a beacon of hope, reminding me of the unwavering presence of faith in my life. They have been like a warm embrace, offering comfort and reassurance that even in the midst of trials, there is purpose and growth. The words of Psalm 23, "Even though I walk through the darkest valley, I will fear no evil, for you are with me," echo the sentiment that we are never truly alone in our journeys. This verse, with its imagery of divine companionship, reassures us that there is guidance and protection even when the path seems shadowed by doubt.

In embracing these scriptural reflections, I have found that faith can transform the way we perceive our struggles. Just as the winter prepares the earth for the vibrancy of spring, our challenges refine and strengthen our spirits, paving the way for new beginnings. The trials we endure become testimonies of resilience, opportunities to deepen our trust in a higher plan, and to cultivate a heart that is open to the lessons of love and perseverance.

As we navigate through our personal winters, let us hold onto the promise of scripture, allowing it to light our path and guide us towards the warmth of renewal. In these sacred words, we find the courage to face the coldest days, knowing that beyond the frost lies the potential for a brighter, more fruitful season.

Sonnet of Stillness and Strength

Charles E. Cravey

The frost has settled deep upon the land,

And silence wraps the world in solemn grace.

No bloom remains, no warmth at winter's hand—

Yet still, the soul finds strength in such a place.

The trees stand bare, their branches etched in sky,

Like prayers lifted from a quiet heart.

Though bitter winds may howl and shadows lie,

The light within refuses to depart.

For trials shape the spirit's hidden core,

And solitude becomes a sacred space.

What once was lost returns with something more—

A deeper faith, a gentler, wiser face.

So let the cold remind you to be still—

For even winter bends to heaven's will.

Blessing: A Benediction for Winter's Soul

May the hush of winter bring peace to your spirit,

And the cold remind you of the warmth within.

May your trials be tempered by grace,

And your solitude become a sanctuary.

May you find strength in stillness,

Hope in the frost,

And the quiet assurance that spring will come.

Go forth, beloved, wrapped in resilience and light.

Chapter 6

The Cycles of Seasons

Embracing Change

Understanding Cycles: Embracing Inevitable Change

Life is an intricate dance of cycles, an ever-revolving journey through the seasons that shape our experiences and perspectives. Much like nature transitions from the vibrancy of spring to the quietude of winter, we too undergo profound transformations as we navigate through life. Each phase—whether it be joy or sorrow, growth or decay—holds within it essential lessons, urging us to embrace change rather than resist it.

"To everything there is a season, and a time to every purpose under the heaven." —Ecclesiastes 3:1

Change is often met with apprehension; we fear the unknown, clinging to the familiarity of what once was. Yet, it is precisely within these cycles that our resilience is forged, and our character is sculpted. To truly live is to acknowledge that everything is temporary, that moods shift, opportunities arise and fade, and that even rays of sunshine follow the most devastating storms. Embracing change empowers us to adapt, grow, and become more attuned to the rhythm of life.

"The Quilt of Seasons":

I once sat with my mother as she stitched a quilt from scraps of old clothing—each square a memory, each thread a story. There was my father's flannel shirt, worn during long walks in autumn. A swatch from my childhood Easter shirt, soft and pastel like spring. Even a patch from a summer picnic blanket, faded but still fragrant with joy.

As she worked, she spoke of seasons—not just the weather, but the seasons of our souls. "You don't throw away the hard winters," she said. "You stitch them in. They hold the warmth in place."

Renee and I still have that quilt. It reminds us that life isn't a straight line—it's a spiral, a dance, a tapestry. And every season, no matter how fleeting or difficult, belongs in the pattern.

It is in these moments of transition that we discover our true strength and capacity for renewal. The process of change encourages us to remain open-minded and flexible, allowing us to thrive in the face of uncertainty.

As we journey through life's seasons, we learn to find beauty in the ephemeral—the fleeting moments that, while transient, leave lasting imprints on our souls. The gentle whisper of autumn leaves, the crisp bite of winter air, the fragrant promise of spring blooms, and the radiant warmth of summer sun all serve as reminders of life's impermanence and its inherent beauty.

"Life is a series of natural and spontaneous changes. Don't resist them—that only creates sorrow. Let reality be reality." —Lao Tzu

By fully embracing the cyclical nature of existence, we cultivate a deeper understanding of ourselves and the world around us. We become more adept at navigating life's challenges, finding solace in the knowledge that each phase, no matter how daunting, carries with it the seeds of new beginnings. In this way, we are not just passive observers of change but active participants in the dance of life, joyfully stepping into the unknown with courage and grace.

Life Experiences: The Seasons as a Tapestry

Each season represents a unique chapter in the grand narrative of our lives, contributing to a rich tapestry woven from countless experiences.

"The only thing that makes life possible is permanent, intolerable uncertainty; not knowing what comes next." —Ursula K. LeGuin

"Spring", with its fresh blooms and burgeoning growth, symbolizes new beginnings and endeavors. It is a time of awakening, a period ripe for ambition and reinvention. This season encourages us to harness our hopes and dreams, reminding us that with every end comes the promise of new possibilities.

"Summer" follows, bursting forth with warmth and vibrancy. It embodies the midpoints of our journeys—times filled with abundant energy, celebration, and connection. We find ourselves surrounded by loved ones, forming bonds that nourish our spirits and fill our hearts with joy. Yet, as the sunlight blazes down, it also reminds us to cultivate balance and care for our well-being.

As "Autumn" approaches, we witness a slow descent into introspection. The leaves transition to shades of gold and crimson, echoing the beauty found in letting go. This season teaches us the importance of reflection—of acknowledging what we have achieved while also accepting what must be released. It is a gentle reminder that closure is necessary for new growth, setting the stage for rejuvenation.

Finally, "Winter" arrives, cloaked in stillness and quiet. It invites us to retreat inward, to recharge and restore. Much like nature, where life is not visibly active, we too must recognize the significance of this stillness in our own lives. It is a time for healing, contemplation, and preparing for the inevitable return of spring.

Together, these seasons illustrate the beauty of life's journey; they show us how each experience, no matter how fleeting or challenging, contributes to our overarching narrative.

"The moon and sun are eternal travelers. Even the years wander on. A lifetime adrift in a boat, or in old age leading a horse by the bridle—every day is a journey, and the journey itself is home." —Matsuo Basho

In this intricate tapestry of seasons, we find a profound metaphor for our own personal evolution. Each phase gently nudges us to embrace both the highs and the lows, weaving them into the fabric of our being. As we navigate through these cycles, we gain wisdom and resilience, learning to dance gracefully with the ebb and flow of life.

In spring, we plant the seeds of our aspirations, nurturing them with optimism and hard work. Summer offers us the fruits of our labor, teaching us to appreciate abundance and to share our successes with others. Autumn, with its poignant beauty, encourages us to harvest lessons from our experiences, helping us to shed what no longer serves us. Winter, though stark, provides a sanctuary of reflection, urging us to find peace in stillness and to trust in the process of renewal.

This cyclical journey reminds us that change is not only inevitable but essential. It teaches us to cherish each moment, to find joy in the transient, and to recognize the interconnectedness of all things. By aligning ourselves with the natural rhythms of the seasons, we cultivate a harmonious relationship with the world around us and within us. Thus, our lives become a vibrant tapestry, rich with diversity and depth, each thread contributing to the masterpiece of our existence.

Scripture Reference: Festivals and Cycles in Leviticus

As we consider the cycles of life, we can draw parallels to the ancient wisdom found in Leviticus, which outlines various laws around festivals and cycles. These celebrations were not mere routines of the Israelites; they served as sacred markers in time—reminders of their identity, heritage, and spiritual rhythms.

For instance, the Festival of Harvest (Shavuot) rejoices in the bounty of the Earth, paralleling moments in our lives when we recognize and celebrate our own achievements and gratitude. Meanwhile, the Day of Atonement (Yom Kippur) signifies a time of reflection and renewal, urging individuals to confront their missteps and seek forgiveness before embarking on a new year.

These rituals are a testament to the significance of recognizing life's cycles and harmonizing our own practices with the natural world. In embracing festivals, we participate in a broader tapestry that connects us not just to our personal narratives, but also to the communal stories of humanity.

In this way, we learn to honor and celebrate the seasons of our lives—the profound, the joyful, the challenging, and the beautiful—as we collectively navigate the cycles that shape our existence. Through understanding and acceptance, we can stride forward, fully embracing the change that each new season brings.

By weaving these ancient traditions into our modern lives, we create a rich and meaningful connection to the past while also paving the way for a more mindful present. These festivals offer us a framework for recognizing the cyclical nature of life and provide opportunities for reflection, gratitude, and renewal.

Moreover, as we observe these sacred moments, we are reminded of the importance of community and shared experiences. Just as the Israelites gathered to celebrate and reflect, we too can find solace and strength in coming together with others. Whether through shared meals, storytelling, or quiet contemplation, these rituals foster a sense of belonging and reinforce the bonds that unite us.

Through the lens of Leviticus, we see that life's cycles are not just personal journeys but collective ones, bridging generations and cultures. By participating in these time-honored traditions, we acknowledge our place within a larger story, one that transcends time and space.

In doing so, we cultivate a deeper appreciation for the rhythms that govern our lives, learning to move with them gracefully and with intention. As we continue to celebrate the festivals and cycles that punctuate our existence, we embrace a life rich with purpose, connection, and under-standing. These practices serve as a reminder that, even amidst change, there is a constant—a timeless dance that we are all a part of, guiding us gently through the seasons of our lives.

Sonnet of the Turning Year

Charles E. Cravey

The wheel turns gently, never quite the same,

Each season etched with joy and quiet pain.

Spring sings of hope, and summer fans the flame,

While autumn whispers loss in golden rain.

Then winter comes with silence, soft and deep,

A time to rest, to gather, and to mend.

Yet even in the hush, the roots still keep

The promise that the cycle will not end.

For life is not a line, but looping grace,

A sacred rhythm pulsing through the years.

We learn to dance, to stumble, to embrace—

To hold both laughter and our tender tears.

So let the seasons shape your soul anew,

Each turn revealing something strong and true.

A
Benediction
for the
Turning Year

May you walk with courage through each season's
change,

Trusting the rhythm that guides your soul.

May spring awaken your dreams,

Summer nourish your joy,

Autumn teach you to release,

And winter offer you rest.

May you find meaning in every moment—

Even the fleeting, even the uncertain.

May your life become a tapestry of grace,

Woven with wisdom, wonder, and love.

Go forth, beloved, into the dance of days—

Held by the One who never changes,

Even as all things turn.

Chapter 7

Seasons of Community

Interconnectedness

Importance of Relationships

As the rhythms of nature shift, so too do the dynamics of our lives and the people around us. The seasons—spring's rebirth, summer's vibrancy, autumn's reflection, and winter's rest—provide profound metaphors for the cycles of relationship and community. Our connections with family, friends, and the wider community are influenced by these seasonal changes, as they create opportunities for bonding, support, and growth.

"What is the city but the people?" —*William Shakespeare,*
Coriolanus

In spring, we often experience new beginnings—births, graduations, and weddings bring families and friends together, fostering a sense of excitement and hope. This season highlights the importance of nurturing relationships, where individuals come together to celebrate new phases of life. For example, during a family member's graduation, friends and relatives gather not only to show their support but also to strengthen the bonds of community. The joy shared in these moments reinforces the idea that relationships are essential to personal and collective growth.

Summer embodies the fullness of life, where friendships often deepen through shared experiences—beach outings, picnics, or community festivals. It is a time for collaboration and connection, demonstrating how we can draw strength from one another. One summer, I witnessed a neighborhood pull together to revitalize a community park. Families organized barbecues and fundraisers, uniting in their efforts to create a safe and joyous

space for all. This collaborative spirit highlights how interdependence flourishes in the vibrant warmth of this
season, allowing us to witness the impact of collective
action.

*"When you reap the harvest of your land, do not reap to
the very edges of your field or gather the gleanings of your
harvest. Do not go over your vineyard a second time or
pick up the grapes that have fallen. Leave them for the
poor and the foreigner. I am the Lord your God."*

—Leviticus 19:9—10

Autumn, with its beautiful array of colors and the fading
warmth, evokes reflection. As we prepare for the coming winter, we are reminded of the transient nature of
relationships and the importance of gratitude. During
this season, I recall a time when I faced personal challenges; friends organized a "gratitude gathering," where
we shared what we were thankful for—both the highs and
lows. This experience of vulnerability brought us closer
together, emphasizing that even in the darker seasons
of life, our relationships can be a source of light and
strength.

Winter brings rest and contemplation, reminding us that relationships also require time for nurture and rest. As the cold sets in, families gather indoors, sharing stories by the fire. This quiet season encourages deepening connections through shared experiences of warmth and love. Community events like holiday dinners or volunteering at shelters during the festive season reinforce our responsibilities to one another.

Here, a story comes to mind of a friend who, facing financial hardship, received support from their community in the form of meals and shared resources. This season can indeed reveal our capacity for compassion and generosity, echoing the timeless truth that we are stronger together.

As the seasons cycle, they teach us invaluable lessons about maintaining and nurturing our relationships. Each phase, whether steeped in the vibrancy of summer or the quietude of winter, reminds us of the ever-present need for connection and compassion. They serve as gentle reminders that just like nature, our relationships require tending, patience, and care to flourish.

"A single arrow is easily broken, but not ten in a bundle."
—Japanese Proverb

As we journey through these seasons, we learn that growth and change are constants, urging us to adapt and embrace the present while cherishing memories of the past. The shared experiences, whether joyous or challenging, weave a tapestry of support that binds communities together. By understanding the significance of each season, not only in the natural world but also in our interpersonal connections, we cultivate a deeper appreciation for the role that relationships play in enriching our lives.

One summer, I witnessed a neighborhood pull together to revitalize a community park. Families organized barbecues and fundraisers, uniting in their efforts to create a safe and joyous space for all. This collaborative spirit highlights how interdependence flourishes in the vibrant warmth of this season, allowing us to witness the impact of collective action.

Let us carry forward the wisdom of the seasons—celebrating new beginnings, nurturing bonds through shared endeavors, reflecting with gratitude, and caring for one another in times of need. In doing so, we honor the profound interconnectedness of our lives, crafting communities that are resilient, compassionate, and ever evolving.

Life Experiences

From these seasonal transitions, we glean invaluable life lessons about the importance of support and collaboration. The milestones we celebrate together are interwoven with the moments of struggle we endure side by side. Each season invites us to lean into our networks of family, friends, and community—inviting a rich tapestry of experiences that teach us about resilience and interconnectedness.

The wisdom gained from these shared experiences is profound, often shaping our perspectives and strengthening our bonds. As we navigate life's highs and lows, we learn to appreciate the beauty of collective strength, where everyone contributes to the greater whole. In spring, the renewal of life mirrors our own potential for growth and transformation, reminding us of the power of starting anew.

Summer encourages us to bask in the warmth of companionship, where laughter and joy are multiplied through community engagement and shared adventures. It is a season of abundance, underscoring the joy found in togetherness and the empowerment that comes from mutual support.

Autumn's reflective nature prompts us to acknowledge and cherish the people who stand by us through thick and thin. The falling leaves symbolize the shedding of old burdens, allowing us to focus on gratitude and the enduring strength of our relationships. This season teaches us to appreciate the present and learn from the past, enhancing our resilience and capacity for empathy.

Winter's quietude is a reminder of the need for rest and introspection, offering an opportunity to nurture our closest connections. The long, cold nights are softened by the warmth of shared stories and the kindness extended to one another. This season highlights the importance of giving and receiving support, demonstrating how even the smallest acts of kindness can light up the darkest days.

Together, these seasonal experiences form a cycle of learning and growth. They encourage us to build communities filled with love and support, where every member is valued and every voice matters. By embracing the lessons of each season, we cultivate a life enriched by meaningful relationships and a deeper sense of belonging.

Scripture Reference

Connecting these relational dynamics to scripture, the book of Leviticus in the Old Testament underscores the divine expectation of community living and responsibilities towards one another. In Leviticus 19:9-10, we find guidelines for caring for the marginalized:

"When you reap the harvest of your land, do not reap to the very edges of your field or gather the gleanings of your harvest. Do not go over your vineyard a second time or pick up the grapes that have fallen. Leave them for the poor and the foreigner. I am the Lord your God."

This passage invites us to consider our communal responsibilities, especially towards those who are less fortunate. Just as nature has its seasons, our lives are marked by times of plenty and times of need. The practice of leaving portions of the harvest for the marginalized resonates with the essence of interconnectedness—reminding us that in the tapestry of community, everyone plays a vital role.

Leviticus teaches us that caring for one another is not merely an option but a command. As we navigate the various seasons of our lives, may we embody this spirit of generosity and support, recognizing that true community thrives on the foundation of shared responsibilities and love. Here's to embracing each season wholeheartedly, cultivating relationships that nurture our souls and uplift those around us.

Reflecting on the teachings of Leviticus, we see a timeless call to generosity and empathy. This ancient wisdom aligns beautifully with the cyclical nature of the seasons, reminding us that just as the earth provides abundantly, so should we extend our abundance to others. By honoring these principles, we are not only fulfilling a spiritual duty but also enhancing the fabric of our communities.

In a world often driven by individual pursuits, the scripture invites us to shift our focus towards collective well-being. It encourages us to look beyond our own fields, recognizing that our actions can significantly impact the lives of those around us. As we strive to live in harmony with our neighbors, let us be guided by the values of compassion, justice, and generosity.

Through this lens, every act of kindness—whether offering a helping hand, sharing resources, or simply being present for one another—becomes a sacred act of community building. These efforts ensure that no one is left behind, fostering a sense of belonging and unity.

As we carry these lessons forward, let us challenge ourselves to create an environment where everyone feels supported and valued. By doing so, we not only honor the teachings of scripture but also contribute to a world that reflects the beauty and interconnectedness of the seasons themselves. May our lives be a testament to the enduring power of love and community, shining brightly through every season we encounter.

Sonnet: The Tapestry of US

Charles E. Cravey

In spring we gather, hearts in bloom anew,

With laughter rising like the morning sun.

In summer's heat, our bonds are tried and true,

Through shared delight and work that must be done.

When autumn calls, we pause to count the cost,

Of time and trials, blessings we have known.

In winter's hush, we mourn what may be lost,

Yet find in quiet love we're not alone.

Each season turns, a thread within the weave,

Of kin and kindred, strangers turned to friends.

We learn to hold, to give, to let, to grieve—

And trust the grace that mends what never ends.

So let our lives be stitched with sacred care,

A quilt of mercy, warm and always there.

Blessing: A Benediction of Belonging

May your days be woven with kindness,

And your nights wrapped in the warmth of shared stories.

May spring bring new friendships,

Summer deepen your joy,

Autumn teach you gratitude,

And winter reveal your strength.

May you never walk alone—

But always within the circle of grace,

Where love is planted, nurtured, and passed on.

Go forth, beloved, into the seasons of community,

And be the blessing you seek.

Seasons
of
Community

Chapter 8

Timeless Lessons from Every Season

Reflections on Lessons Learned

Each season of life brings unique challenges and opportunities that shape who we are and who we are becoming. Understanding these lessons can propel us towards continuous growth.

"All things are in flux." —Heraclitus

1. Spring: Renewal and Growth

Key Lesson: Embrace change. Just as nature renews itself, we too can embark on fresh beginnings. This season teaches us the importance of adaptability and the power of new opportunities.

Application: When faced with change, try to let go of fear and welcome the unknown as a chance for personal development.

Spring encourages us to plant seeds of intention, nurturing them with optimism and care as they blossom into new ventures and insights. It's a reminder that every ending is merely a precursor to a new chapter filled with potential and growth.

By embracing the lessons of Spring, we open ourselves up to rejuvenation and the endless possibilities that lie within the cycle of life. Whether it's starting a new project, building relationships, or exploring uncharted paths, Spring invites us to awaken our senses to the beauty of transformation and the joy of beginning anew.

"The wise man does not expose himself needlessly to danger, since there are few things for which he cares

sufficiently; but he is willing, in great crisis, to give even his life—knowing that under certain conditions it is not worthwhile to live." —Aristotle

Consider taking time this season to reflect on areas of your life that may benefit from a fresh perspective. Engage in activities that spark curiosity and creativity, allowing yourself to explore new horizons without the constraints of past expectations.

"The journey is essential to the dream." —St. Teresa of Avilia

2. Summer: Abundance and Joy

Key Lesson: Cherish your victories. Summer is a time of abundance, reminding us to celebrate our achievements, no matter how small. It teaches us to find joy in the present moment.

Application: Take time to acknowledge your accomplishments and share joy with others, fostering a support system that uplifts you.

Celebrate the warmth of connections and the richness of experiences that this season brings. Summer invites us to bask in the glow of our successes and to appreciate the journey that brought us here. It's a season of fullness and vibrancy, where the days are long and filled with opportunities for laughter, adventure, and relaxation.

Embrace the sunlight not only as a source of physical warmth but as a metaphor for the light within you. Use this time to recharge your spirit, engage in activities that bring you happiness, and surround yourself with people who contribute positively to your life. Allow the energy of summer to inspire you to live fully and authentically, savoring each moment as it comes.

Consider taking part in community events, outdoor activities, or simply spending time with loved ones under the open sky. These moments of joy and connection can strengthen bonds and create cherished memories that last a lifetime. Remember that abundance isn't about material wealth but also about the richness of experiences and relationships.

As summer unfolds, take a moment to reflect on the goals you've achieved and the progress you've made. Celebrate your journey with gratitude, acknowledging that each step forward is a testament to your hard work and dedication. By appreciating the abundance in your life, you nurture a mindset of positivity and contentment, paving the way for continued growth and happiness.

"The seasons are what a symphony ought to be: four perfect movements in harmony with each other."
—Arthur Rubinstein

3. Autumn: Reflection and Letting Go

Key Lesson: Understand the importance of letting go. Autumn signifies the shedding of leaves, much like how we must release things that no longer serve us to make space for new growth.

Application: Reflect on what aspects of your life no longer align with your goals. Release them with gratitude for the lessons they provided.

Autumn encourages introspection, inviting us to take stock of our lives and identify areas that may need change. As the world around us transitions into a palette of warm hues, it serves as a visual reminder that transformation is a natural and necessary part of life.

This season teaches us the beauty of release, showing us that letting go is not a loss but a step towards renewal. By shedding the old, we make room for the new—new experiences, new insights, and new paths that align more closely with our true selves.

"Your word is a lamp for my feet, a light on my path."
—Psalm 119:105

Consider using this time to evaluate personal goals, relationships, and habits. Ask yourself: What is holding me back? What can I let go of to move forward? This process can be both liberating and enlightening, helping you to focus on what truly matters.

Take this opportunity to engage in rituals of release, such as journaling, meditation, or simply spending time in nature, allowing the calming energy of autumn to guide you. As you let go of what no longer serves you, embrace the sense of peace and clarity that comes with it.

Autumn is a gentle reminder that change is inevitable and that by embracing it, we can grow stronger and more resilient. It's an invitation to trust in the cycle of life and to find comfort in the fact that each end is simply the beginning of something new.

4. Winter: Rest and Resilience

Key Lesson: Embrace rest and introspection. Winter calls us to slow down, recharge, and seek inner strength during times of hardship.

Application: Use this season to delve into self-reflection and prepare yourself mentally and emotionally for future challenges...

Winter invites us to embrace the quiet and stillness, allowing us to turn inward and find clarity amidst the cold. It's a time to honor rest as an essential component of resilience, understanding that periods of dormancy are crucial for future growth.

In these colder months, give yourself permission to pause and reflect on your journey. Take advantage of the longer nights to engage in introspective practices such as journaling or meditation. These moments of solitude can reveal deeper insights and foster a sense of peace and acceptance.

Consider this season as an opportunity to cultivate inner strength. Just as nature conserves its energy to withstand the chill, you too can build your resilience by nurturing your mental and emotional well-being. Prioritize self-care, whether through cozying up with a delightful book, enjoying a warm bath, or simply taking time to breathe and be present.

Winter also teaches us the beauty of simplicity. Stripped of the distractions of busier seasons, it encourages us to appreciate the small comforts—a warm meal, a heartfelt conversation, the stillness of a snowy day. Let these moments remind you of the richness found in life's quieter aspects.

"You are my refuge and my shield; I have put my hope in your word." — Psalm 119:114

As you prepare for the emergence of Spring, use this time to set intentions for the year ahead. Reflect on the lessons learned from the past seasons and consider how they can guide your path forward. Trust that the rest and reflection of Winter will equip you with the strength and clarity needed to embrace the coming changes with grace and optimism.

In honoring the lessons of Winter, remember that resilience is not just about enduring challenges but also about emerging renewed and ready to thrive. Each season, with its unique wisdom, contributes to your personal tapestry, weaving a story of growth, learning, and transformation.

As you journey through these seasons, remember that each stage is an integral part of life's tapestry, weaving together experiences that contribute to your growth and understanding.

- **Embrace the Cycle:** Life is cyclical. Much like the seasons, your personal growth is a continuous journey. Embrace the ebb and flow, knowing that each phase brings its own set of lessons.

- **Celebrate Progress:** Acknowledge not just the major milestones, but also the small steps that lead you forward. Every achievement, big or small, is a testament to your resilience and determination.

- **Practice Patience:** Growth takes time. Just as seeds planted in spring take months to flourish, your personal developments require patience and nurturing.

In embracing these lessons from each season, you cultivate a deeper appreciation for life's journey and the wisdom it imparts. Let these insights guide you with grace and fortitude, as you navigate through the ever-changing seasons of your own life.

Life Experiences: Practical Advice and Encouragement

Years ago, I began keeping a seasonal journal—not just of weather or events, but of thoughts, prayers, and lessons. In spring, I wrote of hope and new beginnings. In summer, I recorded laughter and long walks with loved ones. Autumn brought pages of reflection, and winter, quiet entries of grief and grace. Over time, I saw patterns emerge—not just in nature, but in my soul. The journal became a mirror, showing me that growth is not linear, but layered. That joy and sorrow often walk hand in hand. And that each season, no matter how brief or bitter, leaves behind a gift.

Navigating life's seasons requires both practical strategies and a resilient mindset. Here are some tips to help along the journey.

Stay Flexible: Life rarely goes as planned; remaining adaptable can make transitions smoother. Just like a tree bends with the wind, be willing to adjust your expectations.

Build a Support Network: Surround yourself with individuals who inspire and uplift you. Healthy relationships can provide comfort and guidance through life's difficulties.

Practice Gratitude: Regularly acknowledging the positives in your life can shift your perspective and foster resilience. Keep a gratitude journal to document the blessings of each season.

Set Realistic Goals: Allow your ambitions to evolve as you grow. Each season has its unique pace; set goals that respect this rhythm.

Seek Wisdom: Investigate books, mentors, and experiences that offer insights. They can guide you through uncertain waters, enriching your journey.

Embrace Change: Accept that change is inevitable and often leads to growth. Viewing change as an opportunity rather than a setback can open new doors and provide fresh perspectives.

- **Cultivate Mindfulness:** Being present in each moment allows you to fully experience life's offerings, whether joyful or challenging. Mindfulness practices can help you stay grounded and reduce stress.

- **Prioritize Self-Care:** Taking care of your physical, mental, and emotional well-being is crucial. Set aside time for activities that rejuvenate you, ensuring you have the energy to face life's challenges.

- **Reflect Regularly:** Periodic reflection helps you stay aligned with your values and goals. Consider keeping a journal to track your thoughts and growth over time.

- **Find Joy in Simplicity:** Appreciate the simple pleasures in life, from a sunrise to a warm cup of tea. These moments can bring immense joy and remind you of the beauty in everyday life.

By incorporating these strategies into your life, you nurture a mindset that is both resilient and open to the lessons each season offers. Remember, your journey is uniquely yours, and every step is a testament to your strength and perseverance.

Scripture Reference

To conclude, let us reflect on the wisdom found in Psalm 119, which encourages us to strive for righteousness while holding onto hope and perseverance:

Psalm 119:114: "You are my refuge and my shield; I have put my hope in your word."

This verse beautifully encapsulates the essence of finding sanctuary and strength in faith. It reminds us that amidst life's uncertainties, there is a protective presence that offers comfort and hope. This assurance becomes a guiding force, helping us navigate through both the trials and triumphs of each season.

As you reflect on this scripture, consider how the concept of refuge can manifest in your own life. It might be through the support of loved ones, the peace found in nature, or the quiet moments of introspection that provide clarity and direction. Embrace these sources of strength, allowing them to shield you from life's storms and nourish your spirit.

Let this passage encourage you to trust in the enduring power of hope. Just as a shield guards against external forces, your hope can protect your heart and mind, fostering resilience and courage. By placing trust in this hope, you empower yourself to face challenges with a steadfast spirit, knowing that you are never truly alone.

As you integrate these insights into your journey, may you find solace in the knowledge that you are held by a force greater than yourself—one that offers unwavering support and guides you toward a future filled with promise and possibility.

Psalm 119:105: *"Your word is a lamp for my feet, a light on my path."*

This verse offers a profound reminder of the guidance and clarity that faith can provide us throughout our life's journey. Just as a lamp illuminates the way in the darkness, these words can serve as a source of enlightenment, helping to navigate the uncertainties and decisions that lie ahead.

As you reflect on this scripture, consider how it resonates with your own experiences. In times of doubt or confusion, let this message reassure you that there is always a guiding light to lead you towards understanding and purpose. It invites you to trust in the path that is unfolding before you, even when it seems unclear, knowing that every step is part of a greater journey.

Let this be a reminder to seek wisdom and inspiration not only from sacred texts but also from the world around you. Whether it's through the beauty of nature, the kindness of others, or the quiet moments of reflection, there are countless ways to find the light that guides your path.

Embrace this illumination as a symbol of hope and direction and allow it to inspire you to move forward with confidence and courage. Know that you are never truly in darkness, for there is always a light to guide you, helping you to grow and thrive in every season of your life.

Psalm 119:33-34: *"Teach me, Lord, the way of your decrees, that I may follow it to the end. Give me under-*

standing, so that I may keep your law and obey it with all my heart."

This passage beautifully captures the longing for wisdom and guidance in our spiritual journey. It reflects a deep desire to not only learn but to embody the teachings with sincerity and devotion. As you contemplate these words, consider how they resonate with your own quest for understanding and growth.

In seeking to follow a path of righteousness, this scripture invites us to open our hearts and minds to the lessons that lie before us. It encourages us to cultivate a spirit of humility and openness, recognizing that true understanding comes from a willingness to listen and learn.

As you reflect on this verse, ponder how you can apply its message to your daily life. It means taking time each day to engage in thoughtful reflection or seeking out experiences that challenge your perspective and enrich your understanding. By doing so, you honor the call to live with integrity and purpose.

Let this scripture be a source of inspiration as you navigate your journey, reminding you that the quest for wisdom is a lifelong endeavor. Embrace the lessons that come your way, trusting that they will guide you toward a deeper sense of fulfillment and peace.

These verses remind us that even in the darkest seasons, we are never alone. Through hope and perseverance, we can move forward in righteousness, ready to embrace the lessons each season brings. They serve as a beacon, guiding us through the complexities of life with wisdom and grace. As we navigate the cycles of our own journey, these teachings provide a foundation of strength and resilience, encouraging us to remain steadfast in our pursuit of personal and spiritual growth.

By anchoring ourselves in these timeless truths, we cultivate a sense of peace and purpose, knowing that each step we take is illuminated by a light that transcends the seasons. Let these words inspire you to embrace each moment with an open heart, trusting that the path ahead is filled with opportunities for learning, healing, and transformation.

May you find solace in the knowledge that you are supported by a greater wisdom, and may it empower you to live a life of meaning and joy, regardless of the challenges you face. As you continue this journey, remember that the lessons of the seasons are not just about change but about the enduring hope that guides us through it all.

Sonnet of the Seasons' Wisdom

Charles E. Cravey

The springtime taught me how to rise and bloom,

To greet the dawn with hope and open hands.

The summer showed me joy in full perfume,

A dance of light across the golden lands.

Then autumn whispered, "Let the old things fall,"

And colored loss with beauty, bold and deep.

While winter came with silence, soft and small,

To teach me how to rest, reflect, and keep.

Each season carved its lesson in my soul,

A sacred rhythm pulsing through the years.

They shaped my heart, they made the broken whole,

And turned my doubts to prayers, my wounds to cheers.

So now I walk with wisdom as my guide—

Each season's truth a lantern at my side.

Blessing: A Benediction for the Journey

May the lessons of spring awaken your courage,

The warmth of summer nourish your joy,

The wisdom of autumn deepen your gratitude,

And the stillness of winter strengthen your soul.

May you carry each season's truth with grace,

And walk forward with a heart open to change.

May your journey be lit by love,

Guided by faith,

And shaped by the timeless rhythm of renewal.

Go forth, beloved, into the turning year—

A soul seasoned by grace,

And ready for all that blooms ahead.

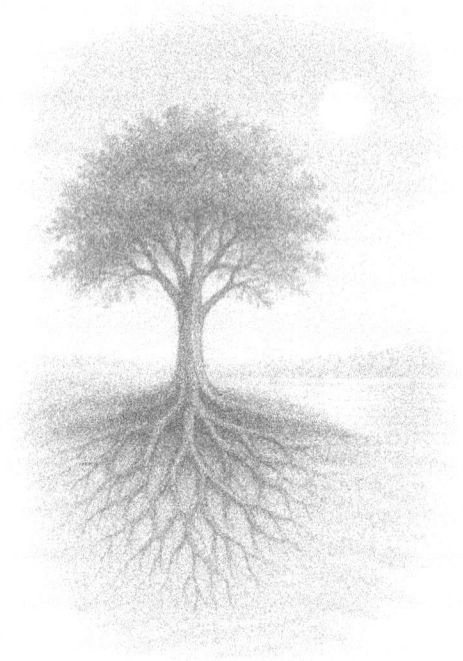

Chapter 9

Conclusion

"See, I am doing a new thing! Now it springs up; do you not perceive it?" —Isaiah 43:19

Final Thoughts: Life, much like the natural world, unfolds in distinct seasons—each with its unique beauty and challenges. Just as spring brings renewal and summer radiates warmth, our own journeys are punctuated by moments of joy and struggle. Embracing these seasons allows us to acknowledge our growth, learn from our experiences, and appreciate the fullness of life. Remember that even in the winter of our hardships, there lies an opportunity for reflection and rejuvenation.

As we close this chapter, let's carry forward the wisdom gained from each experience. Cherish the vibrant colors of your personal spring, bask in the warmth of summer's achievements, and find peace in the quiet introspection that autumn and winter offer. Life's seasons are not merely phases to endure but opportunities to evolve, to find strength in resilience, and to cultivate an enduring sense of hope. Let us approach each new day with gratitude and anticipation, knowing that every season brings its own gifts and lessons.

"Rejoice with those who rejoice; mourn with those who mourn." —Romans 12:15

"He who began a good work in you will carry it on to completion until the day of Jesus Christ." —Philippians 1:6

Call to Action: As you navigate your own path, take a moment to reflect on your personal seasons. What joys have you celebrated, and what struggles have shaped you? Seek wisdom from scripture, allowing its timeless truths to guide you through both the blossoming and barren times. Embrace the cyclical nature of life and find assurance that each season serves a purpose in the grand tapestry of your journey. Let each chapter, each season, inspire you to grow and flourish in your own unique way.

"What we call the beginning is often the end. And to make an end is to make a beginning. The end is where we start from." —T.S. Eliot

Take the insights you've gained and share them with others. Engage in conversations that uplift and encourage growth, fostering a community where experiences are exchanged and wisdom is collectively built. Reach out to those around you, offering support and understanding, as we all traverse the varied landscapes of our lives.

"The best way to find yourself is to lose yourself in the service of others." —Mahatma Gandhi

Years ago, I wrote a letter to someone who had deeply impacted my life—a mentor whose quiet encouragement helped me through a difficult season. I never sent it. I tucked it into a drawer, thinking I'd find the right moment. Years passed. The letter yellowed. And one day, I realized the moment had come and gone. But the act of writing it changed me. It reminded me that gratitude, even unspoken, has power. That reflection is a gift we give ourselves. And that sometimes, the most important stories are the ones we carry in our hearts.

Remember, you are not alone in this journey. Every connection you make strengthens the fabric of our shared humanity. Let your story be a beacon, illuminating the paths of those who walk beside you. In embracing the seasons of life, may you find not only personal fulfillment but also the joy of contributing to a world that thrives on compassion, resilience, and hope.

"The meaning of life is to find your gift. The purpose of life is to give it away." —*Pablo Picasso*

Blessing: Benediction for the Journey Ahead

May the seasons of your life continue to unfold with grace.

May spring renew your spirit, summer fill your heart with joy,

Autumn teach you to release with wisdom,

And winter offer you rest and reflection.

May your story be a light to others.

And your presence is a balm to those in need.

May you walk forward with courage,

Rooted in hope,

And wrapped in the quiet assurance

That every season serves a sacred purpose.

Go forth, beloved,

Not just changed—but changing others through love.

Other Works by Dr. Cravey:

https://drcharlescravey.com or Amazon.com

www.ingramcontent.com/pod-product-compliance
Lightning Source LLC
LaVergne TN
LVHW011207080426
835508LV00007B/649